Ditzy Daisy

DATING
DILEMMAS

*The art of meeting
entirely the wrong man
through online dating*

Dating Dilemmas: the art of meeting entirely the wrong man through online dating

First published by Pica Books, 10 Sydney Road,
Draycott, Derbyshire, DE72 3PX, UK.
Pica Books www.picabooks.co.uk is wholly owned
by Angela Garry *trading as* Pica Aurum.

Edited by Angela Garry.

British Library Cataloguing-in-Publication Data

A catalogue entry for this book is available from
the British Library.

ISBN-13: 978-1517454647

ISBN-10: 1517454646

Printed and bound by www.createspace.com

Dedication

To all the men I've loved before….

Acknowledgements

I'd like to give thanks to my friends who encouraged me to tell everyone...

Not forgetting, of course, thanks to my adorable and amazing friend Angela Garry who turned this into a book in the space of a few hours. She's a true geek!

Contents

Introduction

This book, although written under a pseudonym, contains true stories of the horrors of online dating.

Only first names have been included, to protect the not-so-innocent.

Readers, beware – before you launch yourself on a match-making website, TAKE HEED of those I met on my travels through the world of online dating.

With love

Ditzy Daisy
 x

The Online Dating Dilemma

Internet dating – yay or nay? I say, no way!

It's a bright autumnal Sunday afternoon and I sit here looking back over the five years of off and on internet dating.

What, so long?

I know it's ridiculous but hopefully I have learnt lots… I feel ashamed of my stupidity that is for sure.

I am a clever woman; well I have a degree and not a naff, half-baked joke of a degree like quilting or rowing.

At any rate I also have a Post Graduate degree and now a Masters and still I have acted like a total fool.

In my defence I am also going to blame some 'mental case' males and the strange culture of internet dating that we have embraced as 'normal' – uh oh – do I sound sexist too?

OK, a note about the sexist thing; I was in conversation with some colleagues the other day and we were discussing the pros and cons of internet dating.

One of my young friends was waxing lyrical about a beautiful young ex-colleague who had met a 'handsome, clever, wonderful' man on the internet and she was 'properly' in love.

The advice was for another friend to go on line. I immediately voiced my concerns springing from my own experiences.

Paul said at this stage that he was internet dating and had met many 'lovely and normal' women and was 'having loads of fun.'

My laughing response was: ''of course you're meeting 'lovely and normal' people, Paul, because you're looking for a woman not a man!''

Oh dear… sexist or what?

I would apologise unreservedly because I have male friends who have had strange experiences too but truthfully I personally believe – on the whole – in an uneducated generalising way – that that statement could be TRUE!

OK men, now please prove me wrong and let me know your horror stories.

I came out of a 27 year marriage and instantly flung myself into the 'find a mate; find a lover; find the love of my life; please I do not want to be alone', frenzied search for 'the one'.

Sleepless in Seattle must be true…surely, truly, please say it is?

How my marriage had protected me I was just about to find out…

Bad in Bed James

So the first guy I met on a pay dating website – paying for this service makes it of 'better calibre and more elite', my friends in the know told me – the website that is. It was a reputable website attached to a 'better' newspaper.

James – sorry, I have to have a giggle here just at the mention of his name, in shame at the very thought of my childlike naivety – met me at a really nice pub in a wonderful up market village. He was waiting outside.

I was nervous and shivering a little. I had not dated for 28 years – oh my goodness, my bum was bigger now but after all I was a confident woman who had produced three gorgeous children: I could DO this.

James was tall, over six foot, and bald – a big bald British man! You know the type, not good looking but as I once read, 'a man doesn't have to be handsome, just tall'. He had great big teeth and a big smile.

We chatted non-stop, laughed and I really had a fantastic evening; great start, what can go wrong, I smugly thought? I wasn't really that attracted to him but didn't resist when he hugged me close and gave me a tooth clashing kiss. Yuk, not a great kisser but maybe he is a really nice guy? Let's give him a chance, shall we?

James was overpowering in his enthusiasm – to begin with. Sigh, that seems to be a trend – yup, it can be perfect for a while. "Well", I hear you mutter, "aren't women the same?"

Mmm, yes – I certainly acted damn near perfect, I think: perfect hair, perfect nails, perfect makeup, waxed 'toosh' and legs, listening attentively to every boring detail of his life – guilty as charged. And, oh my goodness, it is expensive and takes up so much time to be this 'perfect'.

The next date was an extremely posh restaurant in Stamford - Jim's Barn – I know the name of the place doesn't sound posh but it is. It's the kind of place where they serve you exquisite food that comes on huge plates and the food looks like a piece of art and leaves you feeling hungrier than when you came in...

All the laughing and chatting, and yet he would not be drawn on anything really serious – no deep conversations about the metaphysical aspects of life. Nothing beyond betting on the horses and what a useless father his father had been – no serendipitous, getting closer connection of the soul moments. 'Getting closer' seems to be a general malaise amongst these dating companions!

This didn't mean he didn't want to get closer to me physically – oh no – that he wanted to do with great bucket loads of enthusiasm. I mistook this for his 'falling for me.' So, sadly (and you are going to sigh a lot at my stupid 'sadly's), I endured his great swallowing, clashing teeth kisses and great squeezing crushing hugs as he apparently tried to make my breasts actually part of his own body. I made the worst mistake feeling in need of physical closeness that sex would mean love – what an idiot!

After a couple of months of convincing myself that we would perhaps grow closer if I hopped into bed with him, believing his sighing 'I'm going to lick you all over,' husky words, and feeling horny after about a year of enforced celibacy and thinking I was in for a seriously super sex session; convinced enough that he really did care for me I arrived at his home 'pantyless,' his suggestion.

Whoa, I thought, is this what had gone wrong in my marriage – I was not adventurous enough? No, upon reflection I realised I had arranged sexual encounters in interesting and exciting places – this could not be it – just James's thing – a little pervy... how exciting!

But, oh! What a let-down! Well not initially. He had great music on, little fluted champagne glasses with delicious bubbly, strawberries... and delicious love making... Oh dear, no! You know the stories we have heard about men with large hands and feet having large 'willys'?

Well, that's all they are – stories. He had the smallest willy imaginable. AND all his breathy illusions of promises of a tongue where we ladies like it – no, nothing – just suffocating me with increasingly repulsive slobbery kisses while he thrust away with his huge pelvis and little sausage.

Of course, he definitely expected me to, wanted me to, desperately wanted me to, go-down on him. Not to be reciprocated though. You know the kind of man who loves sex but not making love to the woman; who loves to play hide the sausage but is not really interested in the women's pleasure unless her excitement is not sufficient to get him going?

I am ashamed to say I faked orgasms to end the torture - was horrified to discover that my wonderful cries and faked shudders did not automatically induce orgasm in the man and he would grin moronically and carry on, content in the idea that he was doing a wonderful job.

He told me a couple of years later that a woman, he had gone on holiday with to Spain, and she had, from what it sounded like, done everything to lure him to the altar. She had told him when he dumped her, that he had a "small dick anyway". James thought that was funny and was slightly bemused when I could not stop laughing. Well done, whoever you are, sister – you had the guts to tell him the truth. Of course, he did not believe that, he just thought it was sour grapes even when I agreed with her.

I began to notice that his desire to go out was curtailed, and more and more his idea of a night out was me arriving at his place and hopping into bed with him after he had magnanimously bought and cooked a Marks and Spencer dinner for two – cost £10.

He had no desire to introduce me to his grown up children or friends but spoke about them incessantly. I knew all about how gifted, magnificent, beautiful, talented, successful – all due to him – these children were. He had no interest in hearing about my three equally magnificent, beautiful, etc. children.

One night after an unromantic banging session which left me unfulfilled but hoping that things would get better (ever the pathetic, desperate optimist), I noticed as I drove past his front window that he was on the internet. Oh yes, he had stopped walking me all the way to my car – just a cheery wave from the front door of his apartment while I made my way downstairs and across the parking area on my own. I knew he was on,line again with that knowledge that comes to someone from the cosmos that he was on the dating website again. Oh dear, follow your instincts!

Now what is so crazy or nutty about this one I hear you say. Well apart from the fact that he was as shallow as a water membrane on the bottom of a glass, after three years he was still contacting me by text every two weeks or so or trying to chat to me on line every time I went on.

I eventually – duh – realised by the timing of his texts and the contents that I was part of his – sorry to be blunt - wank bank! I, eventually, got really, really rude to get rid of him, and I didn't accept calls after 8 pm unless he was in another time zone.

Oh, did I mention he had a very good job in media and I did have some dreams of a lovely life in a nice house in Oundle but quickly realised that I was just a part of his ego stroking collection? When last I heard from him he was still single. He did tell me once that he chatted to another poor creature online, arranged a date with her at a pub only to discover that he thought she was 'ghastly, 'not to his taste at all.' He therefore had one drink and said he was 'out of there.' According to him she had asked him to have one more drink and to please just leave with her so she would look bad leaving on her own. My heart broke for this girl for his heartlessness.

By the way he told me that I had everything, 'the whole package'... yeah, right that's why he couldn't wait to get me out the house after a night at his.

The same day - late afternoon – that I was moving house - yes, folks that's right, he wasn't helping me move. I received a text to check my emails; a brief dumping email about the relationship not going anywhere; well, whose fault was that then? I feel like punching myself: you don't have to roll your eyes at me... I know, pathetic me!

Married to the Mob Andy (or 'Andy nr 1')

The next one was the first Andy – yup, I met several Andy's - and David's - online. Of course this time I found him on a non-paying website. I had tried the paying and that had failed so a non-paying one – BIG MISTAKE! Bigger than James? Well maybe.

The first thing that struck me about Andy nr 1 was his disgusting teeth. In England, why was this man - who drove a large Land Rover Discovery and had his own filming company - walking around with rotten teeth? Why was he on a free dating website, if we think about it? My excuse was naivety... don't be so harsh in judging me!

Andy sat morosely sucking on his beer while I chatted away animatedly thinking a man like this must have some substance – surely?

He then began phoning me at after 11pm, really wild about me. "You're the most gorgeous woman alive; I can't wait to shower everything on you," blah, blah,

blah. He was always a little tipsy. He asked me if I had a great dress as I would be expected to attend film previews and award presentations with him. He would take me shopping etc. He drove me to a village half way between my village and where he lived and told me about the wonderful house he was going to build us.

Yes with a dream of a peaceful life in a gorgeous country house, I would cope with those teeth. Anyway I would get him to sort them later. Was I shallow? Yup maybe, but I was also older, wiser and practical!

Unlike James he arrived and took my young son and I out for lunch; took me to great little country pubs; gave me lovely CD's with good music and all in all seemed OK.

If you're one of those rare creatures that isn't a teeny bit impressed by a smart car and seemingly no problem with money, you are rare and I congratulate you; most of us, no matter how unmaterialistic and generous we may be, are hard wired to seek some sort of comfort.

I felt so sorry for Andy: his wife had died from breast cancer; I could not go to his home right away because his parents were visiting from Spain and they loved her so much that he would seem a kind of desecration for him to be dating, even though she had died about eighteen months before.

Oprah had a TV programme about the 'other women' once. We got to see the other side of the story. A psychologist said that we must not believe that men did not 'understand women.' "No, no" she insisted, "they understand women very well. They know that they only have to bring out the nurturing gene and we're hooked totally." That seems to be true in so many cases.

One evening Andy invited me to the house, saying me that he had something to tell me.

What could that be? He sounded so earnest and serious. We had only been dating for about one month so, although he had spoken about building a house and marriage, I had not taken him seriously; surely he was not going to propose? Now I would get to see his house and see if he was really telling the truth about his money.

My friends all loved the sound of him. He helped me collect a stove from a friend's house – big strong-as-an-ox man. He texted me and phoned me all the time.

(Strangely I was not allowed to have his home number – he made some excuse and didn't answer his mobile but would always phone me back if I had tried but couldn't get through to him.) He wasn't my dream boat but would I find that movie perfect guy? I thought perhaps not.

I had to meet him in the car park of a supermarket in his home town. He arrived and, in retrospect, I realise he was very nervous about me hugging and kissing him in greeting. I followed him to his home and yes, it was a big modern house which matched with his educational movie company story.

Oh, but the house was badly decorated – lots of red, white and black and chrome – not my taste but hey ho this girl could redecorate right? Clever me, brain working over-time. In time maybe something could come of this even though he couldn't converse but his attention and puppy dog adoration could make up for that I thought, sadly.

He sat nervously.

I wanted to laugh. I remember my ex. being nervous when he proposed.

The first words out of this Andy's mouth however: "Don't worry, I'll protect you."

What? My mind wasn't waiting for that statement and I was in shock trying to register.

"Well my wife's family are Irish Mafia and real thugs but I will protect you against them."

Why would I need protection? My brain was totally scrambled and curdled.

"Surely they would want you to be happy? Surely they want you to move on and have a life?"

"Well it will take three months for the divorce to go through and I would like you to stay hidden for those three months."

He just didn't get it – the enormity of his lying breaking news.

Huh my mind was now reeling like yours is dear reader? "Divorced, what happened I thought your wife was dead?"

"Uh no sorry I just said that because I didn't want to lose you." Lose me before he even had any relationship with me – first date? What was that about?

OK, so now I felt totally creeped out. I was alone in a house with a strange man that

I did not know and no one knew I was here.

"So where is your wife now? Does she live here in this house?"

"Yes, but she's at work right now." Totally thick - but how thick was I, getting myself into this situation?

"Oh, my heavens", I thought. "I have to get out" – but I was too terrified to be belligerent and argue with him for his being a lying, cheating, vile and despicable man.

He was not just 'not married' but his wife was dead, according to him, a widow – what a whopper. I had to get out alive – hysterical yes, overdramatic? You be the judge.

I nodded and acted all sweet, desperate to get out of that house. We went into town and he bought a big pork pie for me to take home to my two kids at home. When I got home I phoned him and told him that because of my religious beliefs I was not willing to be the 'other woman' and sorry I could not see him any-longer.

For a couple of years thereafter he continued to send me Facebook friendship requests until I finally figured out how to block him.

By the way his kisses were really bad. I'm not sure about his willy because I didn't get that far – thank you, Lord!

According to him he was also a devout Catholic and even gave me a CD done by some priests that was fashionable at the time.

The mind boggles.

Graham the electrician

I cannot give up, surely I will meet that hunky one; man of my dreams...

While online I met another guy, ten years younger than me; he had phoned once or twice and seemed quite nice. I decided to email him and say 'hello'. Surely I would find the one eventually?

So began my next big mistake:

Graham was also tall. Just over six foot and had a harelip. Aside from this, he was very attractive and had a beautiful body.

How flattering that a man ten and half (don't forget the half) years young than me was so besotted and infatuated with me. He lived far away and so I believed all his excuses to begin with.

I worked sixty miles away from him and one lunch time he phoned and said "come outside and see me". There he was, standing next to his motorbike. He told me he had zoomed up just to see my beautiful face as I made him so happy. Completely flattering and heart softening; sadly I fell for it.

He had a short base Land Rover – what is it with all these guys and their Land Rovers? (But he had good teeth).

Anyway quite quickly he organised that we went away to Matlock for three days. A great break for the two of us. We had a lovely time. Lots of laugher and he was really well endowed… massive in fact.

This time I was convinced: he loved me and ten years in age difference was not a huge obstacle – yippee, he could be the one!

We had a weekend in London and it was beautiful. I couldn't always phone him at night but didn't worry about that too much as he showered me with attention all other times. After all we lived far apart; give that time and it would change eventually I was sure.

Everything was going so well. I had met a guy who had a good job as an electrician, loved my children and they loved him and then - his wife phoned and screamed at me.

I was so shocked!

No way, not again!

What was I to learn from this? The internet is full of predatory men who want sex but are still married?

Well, I have a friend who is on a website specifically for married people to have affairs. Why couldn't and why didn't these two, Andy and Graham, join those sites?

Graham decided that he really loved me and would leave his wife for me. This terrified me because it would mean I was a 'home wrecker.' No way!

He swore he was just looking for love because, "after all Daisy, you know what my libido is like and she would never sleep with me; she hates sex."

I felt sorry for him and felt myself leaning towards him until guess what? His wife became pregnant with their third child. More fool me. I was the 'other woman.' How shameful.

At least now I cannot and do not judge others. Lesson learnt!

Lying Scheming Glen

Right, so I went off men to lick my wounds for a while. The problem is: these dating websites are addictive. Yes, they are.

No one just talks to one person at a time and you end up with an inbox full of men telling you how gorgeous, wonderful, sexy you are. Oh, I defy you to not feel a bit intoxicated by all this attention" Yes, yes I know it is BS but the only way I can analyse it is to say that the reptilian part of the brain takes over and logical sense isn't really in control… no matter how clever you are!

After this I decided it was back to something like Match.com: vet the guy really well, ask him point blank if he's married; make sure I can get a home number and phone him at odd hours… paranoid type behaviour but necessary I reckon.

So I went on several dates thereafter. A lovely heady whirl wind of dating: the type the media tries to paint as 'such fun' blah, blah, blah.

It's the kind of experience that always looks better from an objective stance but the subjectivity of living it is a bit different. I can just see those perfectly manicured magazine journalists telling us all to "go out and meet and date and have such fun". Something they're not doing or speaking to more than two women about – one pro and one against: Never enough real research and information; influencing us, the desperate and searching…

This is not fun, reader.

Don't forget that humans do not like rejection or rejecting and there is bucket loads of that in internet dating – oh, just bucket loads. The good news is you get calloused and somewhat jaded with the rejecting and rejection. How sad!

Around this time I got a really rude message on the dating website from a guy called Glen saying that I could've at least cancelled seeing him and he had waited for me, for over an hour outside the post office in my Village. Erm, what?

I looked at his photo – definitely not someone I was in anyway attracted to; not just this but he had spelling mistakes in his profile – a definite turnoff. When had I said I would meet him? I re-read the messages. Anyway I digress - out of guilt on a snowy day I donned my gorgeous soft leather high heeled boots, white scarf and beret and went off to meet him in the high street of a town near us.

He looked much better than his internet photo. What a relief! We had such a fun afternoon: cream tea at Burghley House, drinks at The George; sitting in front of a fire and laughing. He had a rough accent but his confidence seemed to overshadow anything negative. OK, the teeth again – sorry but too many men have awful teeth! I forgot about that when he confidently grabbed my coat lapels, pulled me bossily to him and gave me a great big smacking kiss. It was strangely exciting. And it was downhill from there...

He drove an Alfa (later a pretentious Jaguar) but had a Porsche which was covered and unlicensed in winter. He was a carer but said he was very clever with money. Well he must've been.

From then on out I was regaled with how much he loved Jane – a woman fifteen years older than him but "oh so wonderful, sweet, kind, gentle, blah... blah... blah," etc. He did say she wouldn't speak to him now because he 'was too dishonest.' Can you believe it? Wow, what had he done? Well, let me see…

He told me about all the wonderful holidays he had taken Jane on and if I played my cards right he was such a 'generous,' 'soft-touch' guy that I might be lucky enough to go on such great holidays too. Oh, this girl who had been starved of the smallest gifts of love was vibulating at the thought of the dangled Venice – woohoo – "please take me, take me, I'll be good I promise…" Oh, sadly shallow again – pathetic me!

"Well I had booked this huge apartment at the Luna hotel Baglioni at over £1000 per night", Glen went on to describe the sumptuousness of the apartment until my mouth was watering and drooling…oh yes me please!

Well long story short he missed the flight, decided to drive overland in the Porsche. Oh, poor thing this cost so much more, so while sitting in St Marco Square he hit on an idea: he ran off to the police station and reported a robbery of all his goods. Good plan, the insurance paid him out and he made up what he had lost. Oh just great my heart felt strangely heavy – not my knight in shining armour. The stories of 'trickery' came thick and fast then:

His sister ordered a washing machine, the delivery service left it at the back door when no-one was home and he and his sister phoned to say it had not come so got another one – ha ha ha – except I wasn't laughing. To avenge his ex-wife and her mean new husband he broke into their house and poured paint in-between their sheets –they still haven't found out who did it. He had innumerable ways to scam – oops – I mean 'work' the system and get benefits for this that and the other, etc. etc. I shall not bore you dear reader with a litany of his 'honest' behaviour. Suffice it to say I could not align myself happily to this way of life.

By the way he also said he was 'brilliant' at everything: the best artist, musician, dancer (OK he could dance quite well); etc.

Now I guess you are thinking that I am being very blasé about all the endings of these soirees?

No, it is never easy, whether rejecting or being rejected; it is always a bit uncomfortable to very uncomfortable.

One date likened it to going into a supermarket and picking up a tin of baked beans but then putting it back because you see another tin just down the aisle. Only problem being that we're not tins we're people with feelings – well some of us anyway!

The Scam Artists

Before I swim you along with me on all my other dating experiences, I would like to tell you about the danger that is now becoming more prevalent; not the tale of the heart breaking, sex maniac, sex addict idiot – no, the big time or small time scam artist. And I met a few...

The Christian widower

The first time I came across the Scam Artist was on a Christian dating website. In retrospect, it was the perfect place for a scammer to find naive, more vulnerable women.

This rather handsome man sent me a message then quickly begged me to go on 'chat.'

He was a newly converted Christian, a widower, had two small children to raise, one mixed race. The pictures were blurry and taken at a distance and I 'squizzed' over them.

I rushed home for the next two nights to chat to this exciting man until the third night he told me that he had to go to Nigeria on business and needed a bit of money to help with the children.

Oh dear! I realised now why he was so interested in what job I had.

I told my son and he looked again at the photos: "Mom these look like paparazzi photos".

He Googled the photos – oh, now, please do not laugh too much at me; the photos were of Guy Richie!

Blast, I felt so embarrassed!

Since then it has happened a couple of times, usually, to be fair, on Facebook. Guys would inbox and use the same format – I used to be very rude to them but now I just delete them.

I have also discovered how to allow only friends to inbox me and not others.

The South African scammer

I was also suckered into joining a South African dating website. I had put all my information on my profile, but not paid to join.

A rather handsome looking man – with a close up picture - sent me a lovely opening email.

My friend Keith told me to be brave and just pay the £20 one off month payment. I help my breath and did it.

Then I was mad because within 20 minutes I knew the guy was a scammer.

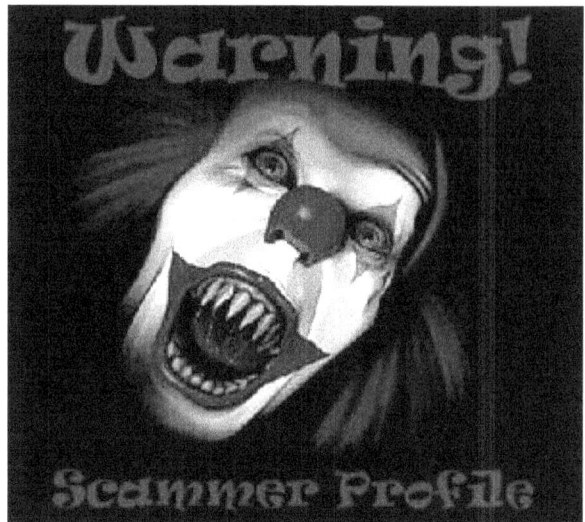

How to spot the scammer:

Here is the basic tick box to recognise the scammer:

- he (or she) is always devoutly religious;
- they are always incredibly considerate of women;
- instead of the whole litany, they beg you to just know they are absolutely romantic and perfect;
- they definitely want marriage and a true commitment to the one they will carry in their hands, close to their hearts forever...yuk!

Rest assured it is invariably some blagster hiding behind his computer anonymity in

Nigeria or some like place – although he will say he is in America / the UK etc.

Be warned: the internet is now full of predators wanting money. And it's not gender specific either – I have heard from my male friends that they are subjected to it as well!

All the David's

I'll lump all the other David's together and see what we get:

Wealthy David

There was David who was wealthy, sophisticated, had a house in London and a country house in a little village near Market Harborough. He confided in me his entire agonising pain about his children, who had gone off the rails, and his ex-wife whom he had adored but had become a lesbian.

"This is the fate of many educationalists", he was afraid – teachers who are such liberal feminists are often "doomed to become lesbians".

Alarm bells went off when I realised he had come out of a three year relationship with another woman and could not commit to her... ah, the non-committal man: there are many about.

It seems strange to me – they're over 45 and yet still feel that they have their whole lives ahead and act as though they're in their twenties with plenty of time to pick and choose and date, and one day form a strong settled relationship which will give them a delightful comfortable old age.

This David admired his own body so much.

He waved down along its length one day and told me to look at how young and lithesome he was – "this body is just not ageing, no wonder I am not interested in women my age."

I was speechless: so many of these men have such massive egos. We can really learn a lesson on self-esteem from them, ladies!

at phillipmartin.info

Lawyer David

Then there was the lawyer David: he had the newest Porsche, and took me to an outdoor theatre. I packed a lovely picnic basket for us and it was a perfect combination of romance and culture.

Well, so I thought, but quickly realised he was only interested in the more animal aspects of relationships... this is all getting so boring with a capital B. No wonder we stereotype men – they are so bloody stereotypical.

The next date was a dinner at a swish restaurant with a specially chosen book for me. What a thoughtful gift. He took me for a walk later into a garden and tried to grope me like a silly school boy.

What do they say about men's car as a penis extension? Oh yes, well it does seem to hold true sometimes – well definitely in the case of lawyer David – once again disappointment – no penis to speak of. I was so disgusting in his selfish, pathetic, fumbling – all about him – sex (sorry it cannot be called 'lovemaking').

I lay there in shock after he came in about three minutes and I couldn't even feel his little 'willy'.

He rolled over onto his back – after ten minutes I put my hand out to try and stroke some life back so that I could have some satisfaction: uh oh – not again – nothing, nada, niks... eeek! I got up, got dressed and left. He had the decency to come to the door with me. I did not want him to come to the car.

I did not contact him but he did text after a day – I could not bring myself to see him again for ages. I eventually did agree to go on a date with this egocentric man (it wasn't just the sex folks – he really was superficial on all levels).

We would go to a Christmas recital at one of the gorgeous churches in a fabulous historic town, on the Saturday night. It had snowed and so everything was picture perfect.

More on this shortly, meanwhile, let's turn to...

Farmer David

I agreed to meet another David (a farming David), from Norfolk on the Friday night. With this sweet, very shy, very boring David we went to dinner at a lovely, open plan, well lit, Chinese restaurant.

There were almost no patrons on this fateful evening when lawyer David walked in with another date and sat two tables away. I nearly died a thousand deaths; funny in retrospect.

Here I was with a date and there lawyer David was with one too and we were due to have our Christmas recital date the next night!

He did text me while at dinner and told me I looked fabulous.

'Delicious' is the word I think he used.

Needless to say I never had the date the next night and the poor farming David I was with was also never seen again – he was really dull - but sweet I am sure.

I used our distance in abodes as a deterrent.

Train-spotter David

Ah, this was the one David who fell in love with me. He came up from London and his main hobby was train-spotting.

He was a truly 'salt of the earth' kind of guy. This David worked for British Airways and was so 'nice.'

I think that his failing was that he was very boring and wanted to be in love without really getting to know me.

He was still living with his wife but according to him separated - I was not taking a chance.

No way, get physically separated or divorced first!

My favourite David

My favourite David was sensitive and gentle but I just could not align my core values to the way he was. I noticed immediately that he had perfectly waxed eyebrows and the shiny skin of a man who had a facial once a week. He spoke sweetly and softly.

His body was slim and lithe and I wondered why he found me, a voluptuous woman, attractive.

He had been married to a Thai woman for fifteen years. His house was immaculate and perfectly decorated. We could not sit in the lounge in case we squashed his cushions. The garden was perfectly designed and manicured.

We were watching a TV documentary one evening on Transvestites in Blackpool. I was amazed and commented that I would love to meet one to get into their brain and try and understand what has enticed them in this direction.

Absolute deafening silence and stillness next to me: uh oh.

The following Saturday he had something to tell me. I was not surprised or shocked at all. He didn't do it anymore; I was really animated about sharing with me what his female persona name had been and showing me pictures.

There is no way I would've mistaken him for a girl – he was offended by that. I gently broke it to him that I could not cope with that – bye, bye love. Here we go again.

I think that may be it for the David's.

It's funny how I met so many of them – but it did make it easy though with not getting names wrong!

Hideous Robin

One of the guys I had been communicating with was a lovely man by the name of Robin. He worked on a commercial ship – something clever.

We met in Northampton at the railway station.

He was docked for a week and wanted us to meet and have a few days at a neutral location. We drove to Warwick and stayed in an average hotel.

He was breathtakingly ugly.

However he was a really intelligent and fun person.

Wouldn't you know it, he had not separated completely from his wife and told me how much he 'had' loved her but since he was not paying her enough attention – blah, blah, blah – she had 'sadly' had an affair – but how could she be blamed?

Sigh, here we go again…

So a few more text messages, some emails and one more attempts at forming a relationship by meeting for a weekend in London and the fizzle was gone.

I did learn something valuable from Robin – do not be scared to do things, people can only say 'no':

We had a lovely morning wandering around Portobello Market – which is way too over priced by the way – but anyway we bought lovely almond croissants. We bought coffee at a lovely coffee shop and he started eating the croissant at the coffee shop. I was mortified, worried about what the owners would say.

He thought I was being ridiculous and I was. They did come over and ask him not to eat it and he said 'fine', apologised and just went on drinking his coffee.

He had not died, no one killed him. It was only a blip and now I am not so ridiculously scared either.

Robin also taught me that the fastest lane in a traffic snarl up is the far outside lane – strange but true.

He did phone me eight months later to say he'd met someone who dumped him after he gave notice on the house he was renting and was ready to move in with her. He felt this was because he had mixed race children and the said lady could not accept them.

Very sad – come on folks, we can't lead someone on up to the point of actually changing their whole lives for you and then dump them – that's just grim.

He was a true gentleman in many ways and met a fabulous lady whom he married about three years later.

Fanatic Andy (or 'Andy nr 2')

Well, now, when am I going to fall in love? All this dating and no love!

Thank goodness it doesn't happen too often, as it is just too dreadful. I decided to be proactive and choose a guy I thought looked good. I saw a guy from Peterborough. He looked lovely in his photo; answered my first contact nudge.

Within a very short time we decided to meet at a bar/pub he knew with good live music. He wasn't quite as gorgeous as his photo and had quite a double chin but he was tall and very manly and just seemed so 'nice'.

He was very confident – very attractive - and bossy – mmm… just what I needed? Really, girl? Oh, had I not learnt yet? Bossy men? Oh, for goodness sake!

We met on a Wednesday night then he organised that we meet again on the Friday evening because although he wanted to see me the next night he had pool on. He was also addicted to Football – yuk – football and pool – not my type and there was me being like a little puppy.

That Friday night I drove to his house and we went to a large beer festival with live music. I do not drink.

He introduced me to all his friends. He seemed so delighted with me and kept looking at me telling me how 'lovely,' and 'adorable,' and 'gorgeous,' and... I was.

We kissed in the crowd while listening to the music for about an hour. It was a marathon. Someone filmed us to put on YouTube and we laughed with delight. Andy was such a good kisser and seemed so romantic because he seemed to adore me so much.

I have no idea – absolutely none – why I fell in love with this guy: I had to pay for myself wherever we went - everywhere.

Ah, I was in love and understood he was poorly paid. But we never seemed to have a very deep and meaningful conversation unless it was about football – sigh.

In an attempt to share bonding memories I asked him about his childhood; he remembers sitting on the curb looking at car hubcaps. Really? Great!

He was mean to my son – covertly mean and wanted to leave him out of every gathering. Unforgiveable of me to have hung on for any more than five weeks when I began to realise this.

After six weeks I got a subversive email saying that he had three types of venereal disease – eek! Strangely it came from his email account which had apparently been hacked and he closed it and opened another account immediately.

After another six weeks, realising that I would definitely be second place to football and pool, I voiced my horror. He immediately decided it was over – thank the Lord! I had strangely fallen in love and this meant I did not sleep or eat for two weeks.

The good things I learnt from him is never put up with anyone being mean to my child at all, I lost weight – bargain – and really stick to your own 'kind.'

If you hate football and pool or if you love it then go for that, or not, but don't try and change your life completely for someone who is just nowhere near the same.

Some of the really strange ones

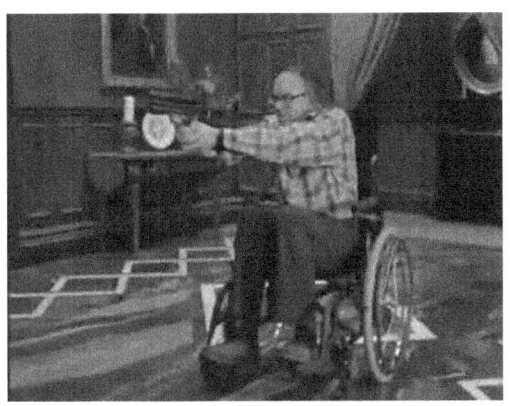

Scary wheelchair man

On a free site – (beware) – I met a guy who told me he was in a wheelchair and almost bullied me into meeting him. I didn't like his personality but trying to be ever sweet and politically correct I met him.

His council bungalow was filthy; he told me how women were falling all over him; they had been to clean up for him but two weeks ago; how much he adored the woman who had recently left him, blah, blah, blah.

I was starting to pray about a way out when he got a surprise phone-call. Oh, I must hurry and drink my tea, he said, (I was petrified because the cup looked grotty), as his friend had run out of petrol and he needed to go and help him – lol – who runs out of petrol in the UK? Yippee!

I was dumped, thank heavens.

58 going on 75...

The next 'strange' one was a man who was apparently a lecturer at Cambridge and 58. He was going up north and could meet me in Stamford at the gorgeous George Hotel. He convinced me he was fine despite a cloudy, poor photo. Anyway

I walked into the very crowded bar and saw no one that I could recognise at all.

Eventually I saw the oldest, grumpiest, looking man at the bar. He looked like a really hard-living 75 year old. I turned to go feeling somewhat relieved when horror of horrors I heard my name; yup, it was him.

He then ushered me into a less occupied bar but there were a group of male revellers – about my age – having a lot of fun. He was maudlin, aggressive towards them, grumpy about the noise.

I could not wait to leave and text him a sweet "not this time buddy". Did he think he could pass for 58, 59? Wow, it's amazing how confident some people are about themselves!

Another odd one was Ray, who also lied about his age. He was really good looking and told me he was 52. He almost passed for that age but for a bow-legged older mans' gait and until I was going through his wedding album and added the date to the year he said he got married – oops – no, Ray, sorry you're 62 not 52!

He immediately shut the album (his wife had died for sure – I had been to his house many times and realised this was true). I felt really fed up.

He also shot himself in the foot a lot because he kept telling me about affairs he'd had but which he was eternally remorseful about.

When confronted with the age thing his excuse was that he was just not attracted to women his age – "do you understand, Daisy?" Yes I do – "goodbye honey!"

The Pervy Truck Driver

One of the scariest dating experiences I had, yes there was something scarier, was a truck driver, who we shall call "M" for the sake of legalities... He seemed OK but after two weeks I realised that he was manipulative and something was too dark about him so I ended it. However he convinced me to stay friends and asked me to go to Huddersfield with him for the day to see his son and step-daughter. I wasn't doing anything and am a friendly amiable person, so I agreed. The day was OK – a bit dull with watching football at a rubbishy pub.

I began to feel strange when I realised that M was 'perving' over his 17 year old step daughter – who looked about 24 with the thickest pancake base I'd ever seen. Apparently she was identical to her mother who had recently dumped him and even (I only found out on this day) got a restraining order against him.

Oh my heavens, my hair was standing up! M stroked her hair and whispered to her. I felt sick. I got her on her own and spoke to her about what was going on. It wasn't good and I can't carry on telling about it.

But I was then dragged into a situation where I had to get involved which was a huge problem for me for months. I envied the people who could just end things and not get involved.

Thank goodness I didn't introduce this man into my children's' lives. Yuk!

Gary from London Underground

By this stage I think I had learnt my lesson and wasn't going to be so 'nice' and affable any more.

I had a date with a chap called Gary who was in charge of one of the underground routes in London. I then discovered these guys earn a lot of money. He spoke with much venom, acrimony and distaste of his ex-wife who had cheated on him.

I just told him that it was nice to meet up with him and I'd love to see him again but then he was not to talk about his ex all the time as it was clear he was still obsessively in love with her – suffice it to say I did not see him again.

People don't like being told hate is still an emotion as all-consuming as love.

Sigh – sads to me – I let a handsome moneyed bloke get away – what a numpty – not!

The Barge Man

If you think that I am a completely silly woman or worse, then let me tell you some stories I have gathered from friends.

One of my friends (who asked that their name not be mentioned) met a bloke – well, shall call him Barge Man – the reason will become clear in a minute. Anyway he was on a free dating website (we all know the names of the most popular).

The picture he put up was of a man with a strong, handsome face. He said he lived on a barge boat near Bath.

They chatted for a few months and then began speaking on the phone – no skype. He sounded lovely, they shared music interest, he had no children, he loved cheese straws; oh my heavens didn't she just love them too.

He eventually managed to convince her to make a four hour drive to visit him for a weekend.

I know, I know – what if he turned out to be the axe killer?

(Remember, dear reader: the internet, texting and phoning dupes us into believing we know the other person. I feel angry as I write this because I want to argue with myself about each person I met online where I genuinely felt that I did know him/her – I'm not stupid – but of course I fell for their words, as we all seemingly do!)

The great day arrived. Driving down she kept glossing her lips, spritzing a tiny bit of perfume and feeling more and more anxious. This feeling grew especially when he texted that "this time tomorrow I'll be serving you breakfast in bed."

She had told him that she needed to have a different sleeping area or would come down later, when she could afford it, and check into a B&B close by.

Barge Man had insisted there were two sleeping areas on the barge and she would have her own bed in her own area – no pressure.

My friend told me that as she arrived at the gate to the barge quay and she saw this scrawny, skrattey looking man walking towards her, her heart just sank.

Oh my lord, he really needed a new pair of jeans.

They reminded her of her dad's jeans when he was an old man, hanging around his hips and buttocks and pulled in with a belt to keep them from falling off. He had a bohemian scarf on, tied around his neck. Generally an interesting look but it looked like a thin piece of rag he had managed to fit and, over a faded T-shirt, it was not a good look.

She could vaguely see a resemblance between the man in the photograph online and this man. He seemed friendly enough and so she felt OK to begin with. She reported to me though that his stories became a bit dark and strange.

Later he ushered her into a Ford Ka to go into town and buy some groceries. She paid for them. Yup, a red flag, I know!

That night instead of going into Bath, a city she had never visited, before they sat holed up in his barge, sandwiched unromantically amongst hundreds of other barges.

Apparently his barge never actually went out on the canal – it didn't have the something or other it needed. What?

That evening he plonked himself half-naked on the bed next to her. My friend said she had no idea what to do but summoned all her courage to ask him what he thought he was doing. He had a huff and stormed off to the front of the boat to sleep in the lounge area.

She was terrified to sleep properly and heard him get up once to pee in a pot near her. Oh my goodness, did I mention that my friend said his barge did not have a loo? Not to worry though, apparently, because there was a Quayside ablution block at the end of a long jetty!

Oh, and she couldn't escape as her car was now parked behind huge Quayside gates – the parking area for the barge tenants.

The next morning would be great as they could then explore Bath. She would just have to survive; scary stuff.

OK, so the next morning he was very sulky; we're not sure if it's because he expected sex or he was just very strange?

He said how sick, physically ill, he was. My friend commiserated and then said that she understood how awful it was to feel sick and have another person to worry about, so she would go home and visit another day. He agreed.

She couldn't believe she made it out alive – frankly, not could I when she told me about the experience.

Please don't judge my friend too harshly – internet dating is a kind of demon that sucks the brightest of us in.

Jane's story: Kobus, the man in love with... himself

My friend Jane (who says I can use her name) told me another amazing story.

She has pretty much had the same strange and now starting to get boring experiences, so decided to look further afield.

Jane was really excited to tell me that she had a cousin who had had great success in meeting a fabulous South African on a SA dating website.

He was handsome – Jane showed me their pictures on Face Book – yup – you got it, they were, well especially he was, very handsome.

They had dated, meet up despite the 5000 mile obstacle and were now eventually married. They even got married in Mauritius; now I ask you, could it get more romantic than that? Nooooooo...

So Jane signed onto a reputable paying site – after the token scammer came along, tried his luck and was duly reported and blocked, then a huge big, rugby playing type guy called Kobus got in touch.

Jane was really excited but like me had a huge cynical hangover.

Kobus was over 6ft on his description – photographs seemed to indicate that this was true. He was quite handsome, not the Prince from Cinderella's story completely, but good enough.

The initial excitement came from how ardently he pursued her. Very quickly he was phoning all hours of the day and night and then, retrospectively, alarm bells started going off: he was telling her how much he loved her; a bit suspicious when you haven't even seen the person for real.

Of course, I suppose it is possible to fall in love long distance; look at Elizabeth Barrett and Robert Browning. Jane, however, wanted the whole Tarzan and Jane experience – well truthfully, don't we all?

Me, I just want a Napoleon and Josephine: complete adoration and devotion. OK, please remember that I often speak tongue in cheek, well, maybe not on this occasion – but mmmm – maybe – it wouldn't be bad, quite nice actually.

Well anyway, I digress...

Kobus wanted Jane, adored her, was determined to be with her; he decided he would come to England to see her.

He then began a bombardment of wanting her to change the venue to Paris, France.

OK, this sounds great but apparently he was getting quite aggressive about it and saying things like: "why can't you make this sacrifice for me?" and "take time off work, just do it!" when she explained that she had a big case coming up and could not go off to Paris for a week. Never mind the cost, etc.

He was adamant and began to be quite bullying. Her gut told her to cancel but she felt duty bound because he had already bought the ticket.

He was a big hotel manager of a resort near Knysner in the Cape. It looked beautiful. She had of course checked this out on the internet and at least this was true.

Her initial anxiety was initially minimised because he arranged a wonderful holiday weekend at a lodge near his resort for one of her children in SA.

Her daughter and friend went along. This daughter phoned and told her he was fabulous: initially left them to settle in then threw a huge barbeque for them; took them to a fabulous breakfast, lunch and site seeing the next day.

He was larger than life and seemed to know everyone. He eventually arrived in the UK.

The first night he and Jane went out dancing to meet her friends. He bought whisky, brandy & coke and exotic cocktails for everyone. The terrible exchange rate did not seem to be a problem at all. Her friends loved him – why wouldn't they?

He did mention that a friend of his had gone to Florida and was successfully in the boat business with a lady he'd met online.

Jane said she thought he might have wanted to emulate his friend in some way with some, more 'exotically' based lady, ridiculous as it seemed.

The vanity of the man was breath-taking. He looked at himself in elevator mirrors and indeed any shiny surface.

He never once told Jane how lovely she looked, an absolute prerequisite for any girl you're dating.

She organised a whole day in London sight-seeing, meeting up with a friend in London's China Town for an early dinner then onto Ronny Scott's for a great jazz evening. What could be better?

Immediately scuppered by his vanity: they arrived and had to spend five hours (I kid you not) in Brentwood shopping centre looking for a shirt to match his jacket.

It was a black jacket, folks.

She took him to a shirt shop based on her impression that money wasn't really a problem. No, he didn't want to spend £55 on a shirt; OK, so off to M&S and H&M and Next and Debenhams and then another shirt shop.

At this stage she took herself off to Starbucks for a hot chocolate and a sulk.

She hadn't even taken her credit card with her from the hotel room, thinking it would be a quick stop. She looked at the other fashionable ladies with their great sandals and wanted to at least comfort herself by buying a lovely pair.

Kobus eventually arrived back with no shirt and took her suggestion to just use a shirt he already had.

He took longer than her to get ready and she had to wait for him outside the lift (she just couldn't bring herself to go to his room). He didn't say anything about the way she looked or even how beautifully she's dressed her long locks.

Apparently he looked at himself preening on in the elevator lift going down and didn't even notice her gorgeous Chinese dress and adorable silky slipper shoes.

OK, so too late for any sight-seeing and they barely made it to dinner. He fussed and to their embarrassment made unnecessary and silly comments about the food. Then onto the Jazz club – what could go wrong? Um, he was morose and didn't speak the whole evening.

She took him to the cathedral and other great places the next day and he barely seemed to notice them saying things like: "ag well ja" (trans. 'ah, well, yes'), "I have good sights in my country too."

"Ag well ja go freaking home" she wanted to say.

It was with relief she put him back on the plane and was shocked that he swore undying love to her. She could not stifle a laugh...

Dear reader you are not going to believe this: after not speaking to him at all a month later she got an email from his secretary asking her to upgrade her Facebook profile to friends only as his WIFE was stalking her on Facebook.

What? Wasn't their marriage completely over?

A few weeks later she got a long email from said wife saying that Jane had broken their marriage up. What?!?

So liars straddle the earth... shock and horror!

The dangerous one: Tony the Plumber

I can't end this diatribe of internet dating unless I mention a horrible plumber I had the misfortune of dating.

His name was Tony and he was a plumber. Now we all know that plumbers are supposed to be loaded right?

Anyway we did the obligatory online chatting, phone chatting/flirting, etc. until we set up a date at a pub/restaurant. He arrived; tall, lean and manly looking with low slung hip hugging jeans – initial impression: attractive.

I was immediately put off as he more than once looked around me to follow the football that was going on, on the TV. I'd already had negative learning from the heavy, intense footballer type – oh dear.

He looked at me in my tight jeans and said I looked good but wished women wouldn't always wear trousers and would wear skirts and dresses more often – I didn't know why he expressed this until later.

I innocently assumed it was because he liked the very feminine look that skirts and dresses give girls. He asked me to meet him for dinner at his house a few days later – I agreed. I wasn't really impressed by him but felt that most people deserved at least two dates.

The next day, as luck would have it, or not, my toilet drain started overflowing. A-ha, I had a second date with a plumber – what luck – how could I go wrong?

I phoned him and told him the problem. He cursed, came over and looked at it without any equipment, moaned about the stench (you would, wouldn't you, especially if you're a plumber dealing in crappy things all day?) and went off having done nothing. I phoned a plumber and paid a lot of money to get it fixed.

Tony managed to still convince me to have dinner with him a few days later – what an idiot, me!

I arrived for dinner in my floaty skirt, pretty lace top, pinned up hair with little bouncing ringlets popping out looking quite romantic, very feminine and dare I say, pretty.

He had a nice house and a good car but as I was pretty hungry I noticed immediately that nothing was going on in the kitchen. Maybe he would take me out for dinner?

He brought me a drink and then pounced on me – kissing lecherously, sticking his tongue lustfully down my throat and pushed me back on the couch. Before I even realised it he had unbuttoned his trousers, pushed my skirt up, moved things aside and penetrated me.

I was so shocked and now realised why he liked shirts. I was too terrified to do anything drastic so just complied as many women do in rape (as I have subsequently found out in anecdotal research).

Afterwards he was chatting away as though nothing had happened, had a beer, shouted out the window to some friend in the street.

As soon as I could I ran home and 'licked my wounds'. He even phoned me a few days later as though nothing was wrong – I truly believe he thought he had done nothing wrong – trying to set up another date.

I had to include this as I discovered something horrible and truly dangerous about internet dating – something that needs to be passed on.

Lessons Learned
recognize mistakes
observe what works
document them
share them

Lessons to be learned

Ladies and gentlemen, it seems that both sexes lie, lie, and lie on the internet.

Their photos are, more often than not, not a true representation and if they are, no one is interested.

It is an unnatural way of meeting; expectations are distorted.

If we have to resort to the internet to meet a mate, then here are some rules I've devised and hope will help you:

1.   Always use a paying website – free ones are just dreadful.

2.   Make sure he/she has lots of photos or he's/she's probably a scammer.

3.   Always meet in a public place.

4.   Make a list of five things to talk about so you're not struggling for conversation.

5.   Go with your gut instinct but be reasonable: not everyone is George Clooney or Heidi Klum.

6.   If they lie about their age, do not trust them.

7.   If you start to communicate by phone make sure you have a landline number for them too to make sure they're not married.

8.   Skype first if possible.

9.   Do not talk about sex as it perverts the intent of the meeting – unless you're only in it for the sex and want that.

10.   If it starts to feel weird; they are a bit off to your children, they are controlling at all or manipulative, or anything else you find abrasive – run, run, run!

11.   Expect some rejection – it's like a jacket – not everyone likes the jacket even if it's a good jacket.

12.   If they start telling you how to run your life – run, run, run!

13. Make sure you are soon introduced to their friends and family, although this is no guarantee.

14. None of the above guarantees anything – make up your own list and good luck!

15. And one last word of advice: if they talk about their ex all the time they are not over the ex - run, run, run!

Normality at last

The tales in this book took place over five years in my life – ending a few years ago. Since then I have at last found the love of my life.

I am quietly seeing a man I met through work and we've been happily dating for several years now.

He's perfectly normal and we're great friends; laugh a lot, quietly do things together and every now and again there's some passion – just the kind of boring, romantic, up and down, fun, silly, irritating, doing things together and on our own and normality that makes for a good relationship – well I think so anyway!

And I'm very happy.

Much love to you,

Ditzy Daisy
 xx

About the Author

Ditzy Daisy is a pseudonym.

(Seriously, who'd have thought it?)

'Daisy' is based on the real life experiences of a 50-something bubbly buxom blonde with a vivacious love for life.